# Lost In Illinois

Discovering Strange and Historic Places in the Land of Lincoln

ETAOIN PUBLISHING
www.etaoinpublishing.com

HURON
PHOTO.COM

Publisher:   Etaoin Publishing and Huron Photo LLC
             Saginaw, MI
             www.EtaoinPublishing.com
             www.HuronPhoto.com




Printed in the United States of America

Paperback ISBN  978-1-955474-15-3
Hardcover ISBN 978-1-955474-16-0
Ebook ISBN 978-1-955474-17-7

A Lost In The States Book
www.LostInTheStates.com

# Introduction

I have traveled all over Illinois from the rolling hills in the north, to the historic cities along the Ohio River in the south. Illinois is known as the Prairie State or the Land of Lincoln, and it is more than just Chicago and farmland. I was amazed at the stories and places I found from inspiring people to tragic events. The twenty-first state has wonderful state parks with nature to explore and historic sights to see. The state also has an important place in our nation's military, both past and present. I enjoyed my time traveling through Illinois, and this book contains some of my favorite locations and stories.

For people on a limited budget, there are plenty of fun and interesting places to visit that are free or cost a small donation. Many parks and historical sites offer the chance for a getaway and are free to explore. If you are willing to be a little adventurous, cemeteries can be fascinating places to visit and also have a lot of stories and history to share. If you are fortunate to be in good physical condition, the forests give people a chance to hike, and some of the trails lead past some amazing places.

This book is not intended to be a "bucket list" of all the things you should see and do in Illinois, but instead, a book containing stories of places, people and things that I found interesting as I traversed the state. Each story in this book is an independent tale about a specific location in the state. You can read them in any order. I do my best to give accurate locations, although some places do not have a specific address, so I give a description of where it can be found. Most places are open to the public and located on public property, but be sure to follow any posted rules, and please be respectful of places you visit. Some places are privately owned and are sometimes opened to the public. Although they may not be accessible, they do have an interesting story that I wanted to share, and I hope that you will be considerate of the owners' privacy.

# Contents

# Chapter 1
## Southern Illinois

# Chapter 2
# Central Illinois

# Chapter 3
# Northern Illinois

# Chapter 1
# Southern Illinois

# Old Shawneetown

Old Shawneetown Bank Historical Site
280 Washington St,
Shawneetown, IL 62984
37.695337, -88.13628

Old Shawneetown sits along the Ohio River not far from the tri-state point where Illinois, Kentucky and Indiana meet. It is one of the oldest towns in Illinois and is believed to have been founded in the 1750s by members of the Pekowi Shawnee

Native American Tribe. After the American Revolution, the United States government set up an administrative center for the Northwest Territory in Shawneetown. Washington, D.C. and Shawneetown were the only towns chartered by the United States government. The town continued to prosper along the banks of the river, and even Lewis and Clark stopped at it on their expedition to explore the lands of the Louisiana Purchase.

Shawneetown had the first bank chartered in Illinois, and it is said that it refused to buy bonds issued by Chicago because it believed the city would never amount to much. It was Shawneetown that never grew into a major city. The Ohio River brought commerce and travelers, but it also brought floods. In 1937, Shawneetown suffered a major flood, and many of its citizens and businesses relocated further inland, starting a new town called Shawneetown, and the original became Old Shawneetown.

A few houses and buildings still remain, but the area seems more like the ghost town of a city that was once started by the federal government. One of the few remaining buildings still standing downtown is an old bank building. It looks rather eerie standing alone while the other buildings that once stood next to it are gone. An old saloon named Hog Daddy's still stands across the street from the bank and is a popular stop for motorcycle riders.

.

The old bank is an Illinois State Historic Site, but at the time this book was published it was closed to visitors

# The Mine Tipple

55 South St,
Muddy, IL 62965
37.76618, -88.51754

The small town of Muddy sits in southeastern Illinois between the town of Harrisburg and Eldorado. It has a population of about seventy people, but in its heyday about a century ago, it was a popular and booming city. On the outskirts of town is a large concrete structure that towers over the small community. It is kind of odd looking with a tall triangular section with large round holes. It looks like some sort of art sculpture, but it was the framework for a mining tipple.

A tipple is a structure used by a mine to load railroad cars. The Harrisburg Big Muddy Coal Company opened a mine in the region, and the town was named after the company in 1903. A few years later, the mine was sold to the O'Gara Coal Company. Everything was great in the town of Muddy as immigrants from eastern European countries came to work in the mine. It all came to a sudden end in 1937 when the middle fork of the Saline River overflowed its banks and flooded the town and mine under several feet of water. After that, the mine closed and most of the citizens of Muddy moved away. The concrete tipple still stands as a reminder of the coal mine. It is open for visitors to walk around it and marvel at its size and shape.

> The former post office in Muddy was one of the smallest post offices in the country. It is a small shed style building and is now a little museum.

# Cairo

Cairo Customs House Museum
1400 Washington Ave,
Cairo, IL 62914
37.002985, -89.171979

Cairo is the southernmost city in Illinois and sits at the confluence of the Mississippi and Ohio Rivers. In the 1830s, it was a prosperous port town with ships stopping to haul goods from the town. Over time, the railroads began hauling more and more of the nation's products, and the popularity of the town began to wane. The town had ferries to transport the rail cars across the river, but it was not long before a bridge was built over the two rivers, and the ferries were no longer needed. In the early and mid 1900s, the town struggled with racial tensions and violence, causing further decline, and after the Interstate bypassed the region, it seemed as if the town was no longer needed. Most businesses have moved away, and few residents remain. Some refer to it as a ghost town, and although many buildings and homes have been demolished or abandoned, some are still standing despite seeing decades of hardship. There are two buildings that stand out in the historic but seemingly forgotten town.

The Magnolia Manor is a large dark red brick mansion with a tower that overlooks the city. It was constructed by Charles A. Galigher in 1869 with the money he made selling flour to the Union Army for making hardtack, a large dense cracker used by troops for food during military campaigns. Although the soldiers may have not enjoyed eating the flavorless wartime cracker, Galigher did well enough financially to build a magnificent house. Galigher became friends with General Ulysses S. Grant when the commander was in Cairo planning his attack on the south. After Grant's presidency ended, a large celebration was given to him at Galigher's mansion in Cairo.

The home has changed owners a few times, and in the 1950s it was purchased by the Cairo Historical Association and now operates as a museum.

At the south end of town is a large three-story stone building known as the Old Custom House. Built at the same time as Magnolia Manor, the building served as a customs house, post office, and courthouse. After construction, it was used to collect tariffs on goods being transported down the river. It was one of the few government buildings designed in the Italianate style and one of the largest federal buildings of its era in the Mid-Mississippi Valley region. After Cairo built a new post office in 1942, the building was used as the town's police station. Currently, it is used as a museum managed by the National Park Service.

# Cave-In-Rock

1 New State Park Rd,
Cave-In-Rock, IL 62919
37.46886, -88.15507

Before trains and trucks transported goods across the country, boats floated cargo down the Ohio River in the early days of the United States. Pirates and thieves often attacked the river boats, and one of the most notorious locations was the Cave-in-Rock along the Illinois side of the river. The massive cave was created a millennium ago by water carving out the rock. It was the perfect shelter for bandits waiting for boats to pass by on the current of the Ohio River.

There have been many tales and legends told about the cave over the past few centuries. Exactly how accurate they are is up for debate. There is a record of treachery and despicable people that used the cave. In the late 1700s, counterfeiters Phillip Alston and John Duff used the cave for a meeting place. They became friends with Samuel Mason, a Revolutionary War militia captain who used the cave as his base of operations. He and his gang of outlaws robbed the boats going down the river. Many of the inexpensive boats were discarded in New Orleans, and boatmen would hike the trail back upstream. Mason's gang would rob them both coming and going. Micajah and Wiley Harpe, known as "Big" and "Little" Harpe, were part of Mason's gang. The brothers were violent and ruthless men, and killed several people in the region. They are considered by some to be the first serial killers in the United States. Eventually, the Harpe brothers and Samuel Mason were captured and beheaded and their heads placed along the river to warn other pirates and outlaws.

The Ford's Ferry Gang made use of the cave after the removal of the Mason Gang. James Ford was a local businessman who owned a tavern nearby and operated a ferry across the Ohio River. He was the head of a gang that hijacked boats and robbed travelers for decades in the southern Illinois and Kentucky region. Local legend has it that the notorious outlaws Frank and Jesse James hid out in the cave, but I am wondering if this is more legend than fact.

In 1929, Illinois purchased the cave and surrounding land, making it into a state park. Today visitors can explore the cave and wonder about all the events that have taken place inside it over the centuries. It was a hot and humid summer day when I visited. Climbing up and down the stairs from the parking lot was a chore in the heat but worth the trip to see the historic cave. Pictures do not convey the immense size of the cave, and even in the summer heat, it was cool and refreshing inside. I can see why it was such a popular place for a hangout. Standing inside of it, I started to reminisce about being a kid in the 80s and thinking of One-Eyed Willie from the movie The *Goonies*. If you get the chance to visit this historic cave, I highly recommend exploring it and experiencing the size and history.

Walt Disney Productions used the site for the 1956 Davy Crockett adventure, *Davy Crockett and the River Pirates*. In 1962, the John Ford Western epic film *How the West Was Won* featured the cave.

# Mound City

Mound City National Cemetery
Located on IL-37,
Mound City, IL 62963
37.08720, -89.178127

The Ohio River town of Mound City was named for the nearby Indian Mounds. The city is home to one of Illinois' oldest national cemeteries. It seems a little out of place for a large historic cemetery near the small town, but at the time it was created it was one of the busiest naval ports in the country.

During the Civil War, the Union had created a naval base at Mound City. Its shipyard built and repaired many Union ships, including some of the first Ironclad ships. The *USS Cairo, USS Cincinnati,* and *USS Mound City* were all built in the southern Illinois town. A large naval hospital was constructed to heal the men wounded in battle. In 1864, land was set aside near the hospital for a final resting place for the men who gave their full measure of devotion to the nation.

Nothing remains of the great naval shipyards in Mound City. A small building and the cemetery are what remain of the naval base from the time of the Civil War.

In 1874, the state erected The Illinois State Soldiers and Sailors Monument in the cemetery honoring 2,637 unknown soldiers and sailors who lost their lives in the Civil War.

# Metropolis Superman

517 Market St,
Metropolis, IL 62960
37.152384, -88.732710

Fort Massac was built along the Ohio River in Illinois during
the American Revolution. It was destroyed by an earthquake in
1811 and abandoned a few years later. A century after the fort

was deserted, a businessman from Pittsburgh and a local landowner worked together to create a new town in 1839. They had a grand vision that the town would become a major city in Illinois. They gave their new town the name of Metropolis. They figured the city would be an important stopping point for all the shipping traffic along the Ohio River. The town did have some prosperity in the early days but never grew to be a great city like Chicago on Lake Michigan.

The city may be small in size, but it is home to one of the biggest superheroes in the universe The Superman comics published by DC Comics claimed that Superman lived in the fictional town of Metropolis. The Illinois town of the same name capitalized on the popularity of the fictional character, and on June 9, 1972, the Illinois State Legislature passed Resolution 572, declaring Metropolis IL the "Hometown of Superman".

DC Comics officially recognized Metropolis, Illinois in Superman Vol 2 #92. In the comic, the fictional villain named Massacre came to the Illinois town in search of Superman, not knowing he was in the wrong Metropolis. The Illinois town has adopted the Man of Steel as one of its own, and a large fifteen foot statue of him stands in front of the courthouse. A

16

museum and other references to the superhero can be found through the city. Each year on the second weekend of June, the city holds its annual Superman Celebration.

A replica of Fort Massac can be found nearby at Fort Massac State Park.

# Herod Cave

 999 IL-34, Herod, IL 62947
37.583345, -88.441449

Il-34 runs north and south through central southern Illinois, and it passes through the town of Herod. There is not much in the little town other than a post office, church and a few houses. A couple miles north of town is a small roadside park and a cave in the rock outcropping. Next to the cave and attached to the rocky cliff is a brick chimney and some crumbling walls. It is what remains of the old Fairy Cliff Cafe, which was open from the 1930s to the 1960s. I am not sure what happened to the building, but what remains of it can be seen in the little park.

It is a nice little place to stop for a break on a trip to the Garden of The Gods Recreation Area in the Shawnee National Forest.

18

# Illinois Iron Furnace

Route 146 &, 34,
Elizabethtown, IL 62931
37.4991, -88.32816

Deep in the woods north of Elizabethtown in southern Illinois along winding forest roads is a large stone pyramid-shaped structure. It harkens back to a time when a furnace was constructed in the 1830s and iron was smelted in the region. The furnace was used until the Civil War when it ceased

19

operating because of labor shortages created when men fit enough to operate the furnace joined the Union Army.

The furnace reopened a few years after the Civil War ended. It operated sporadically until it was permanently closed in 1883. It was the last iron furnace to operate in southern Illinois and stood undisturbed in the state's forest for decades. In the 1930s, it was damaged during road construction. In 1967, the U.S. Forest Service's Golconda Job Corps Center rebuilt the furnace and added a picnic area along with some signage about the historic furnace. It is a bit of an adventure to the old furnace along the back roads, but it is an interesting part of Illinois history and worth the trip to see it.

The forest roads around the furnace are rough gravel roads. I do not recommend traveling them on a motorcycle. I think it is also easier to find the furnace if you come in from the south on County Road 3.

# King Neptune

IL-146 about a mile east of I-57
Anna, IL 62906
37.44571, -89.13195

Near the town of Anna along IL-146 east of Interstate 57 is a small roadside park. There you will find an interesting marker for King Neptune. It is not for the king of the sea but for a pig that helped the greatest navy that ever sailed the oceans. Born in 1942 on Sherman Bonner's farm near West Frankfort, Illinois, he was named Parker Neptune and raised by Bonner's daughter.

The Bonners donated the pig for a pig roast but Don C. Lingle, a navy recruiter from Anna, Illinois, had the idea of auctioning off the pig to raise money for war bonds for the construction of the *USS Illinois* battleship. The pig was auctioned off, but at the end of the auction, he was donated back to Lingle, who took him on to several more auctions where the cycle repeated. Wearing a navy blue cape and crown, he was known by the name of King Neptune, and at one auction, Illinois Governor Dwight H. Green purchased the pig for one million dollars and graciously donated him back. During the years of World War II, King Neptune raised nineteen million dollars for the war effort.

At the end of the war, the famous pig was to be sent off to Chicago and slaughtered, but Lingle felt he deserved better and took ownership of the famous pig. King Neptune lived the rest of his years on a farm near Anna, Illinois. After his death in 1950, King Neptune was buried along IL-146 and a small marker placed in his memory. The marker had to be relocated because of the construction of interstate 57. I wonder how many people have passed by the memorial over the years and know the story of the pig and the money he raised for World War II.

In the late 1980s, the monument was vandalized and a new monument was erected at the nearby rest area on I-57.

# Bald Knob Cross

3630 Bald Knob Rd,
Alto Pass, IL 62905
37.55113, -89.34756

Visitors to the Shawnee National Forest near Alto Pass may notice a large cross standing at the top of a hill. The Bald Knob Cross of Peace has been standing in southern Illinois for over half a century. In 1937, Makanda, Illinois postman Wayman Presley and Reverend W. H. Lirely wanted to hold an Easter Sunrise Service. They chose the top of nearby Bald

Knob Mountain and invited people of all denominations to celebrate Easter with them. The first service attracted 250 people, but over the next few years thousands came to the top of the mountain to celebrate on Easter morning.

Presley organized local citizens and raised enough money to purchase the land at the top of the mountain. During Easter, a large wooden cross was placed at the top of the mountain but Presley had a grand vision for a more permanent monument. He had the idea to erect a large metal cross that could be seen for miles around. Presley began a large fundraising campaign and even convinced farmers along his sixty mile long mail route to raise pigs for his cause. The sale of the pigs raised $30,000 and started the construction of the foundation in 1953. Wayman Presley was featured on the television show *This Is Your Life* and shortly after, the Bald Knob Foundation received thousands of donations in the mail. In 1959, the 100 foot tall steel framework was completed. The white sheet metal was added in 1963, completing the cross.

By the 2000s, the cross had fallen into a state of disrepair with some of the panels falling off and the framework rusting and in need of renovation. Disagreements among the board members lead to lawsuits and the ground of the cross closed by order of a judge. A new group called Friends of the Cross was formed after the resignation of the old board. The new organization oversaw the restoration of the cross and a new welcome center. The large white cross that overlooks the Shawnee National Forest invites visitors from all around the world.

> The Bald Knob cross is not the only large cross to stand in the Land of Lincoln. A 198 foot tall cross stands near Effingham near the interchange of Interstates 57 and 70.

# Foundry House Ruins

Under the Pipeline Bridge over the Mississippi River
Grand Tower, IL 62942
37.64241, -89.51457
(Not Accessible To The Public)

I like to visit the locations I write about to have a better understanding of the surrounding area. When I tried to visit the old ruins I was disappointed that they were gated off and closed to the public. I still thought the story was interesting enough to include, but unfortunately it is not accessible to the public.

The town of Grand Tower sits along the Mississippi River in southeast Illinois. North of town is a rock outcropping that leans out over the river and is called the Devil's Backbone. Next to it is a hill that was given the name of the Devil's Bake Oven. In the early days of the state, it was a popular spot for pirates and marauders to attack boats traveling down the river, and I think that is where the ominous sounding names come from. In the late 1800s, Grand Tower had two iron smelting furnaces, and pig iron was shipped down the river.

On the side of the Devil's Bake Oven are stone walls that once served as a foundation for a house. It is what remains of a house built for the supervisor of a nearby foundry. Known as the foundry house ruins, it is said to be haunted by the ghost of a young woman. I found a few variations of the story, so I am not sure how true it is, but it is a fascinating tale.

The story goes: The superintendent moved into the house with his daughter. He came to the area after his wife died and was protective of his only child and forbade her to engage with any of the men at the foundry. She fell in love with a handsome young riverboat captain, and her father would not allow his daughter to see him anymore and confined her to the house. The man she loved sailed his boat up the mighty Mississippi, and she watched out the windows of the house for his return. The days turned into months, and his ship never returned. When she inquired about the missing ship, she learned that the boilers had exploded and the crew, including the captain, had perished. Eventually, the young woman died either of a broken heart or a deadly illness, and now her spirit is eternally tied to the house where she waited for her sailor's return.

There are different variations of the story and I am not sure if there is any truth to it, but the ruins of a house still stand next to the Devil's Bake Oven. The area is now the Devil's Backbone Park and campground. Unfortunately, when I visited, the road that leads to the ruins was gated and closed to the public to protect the pipeline bridge over the Mississippi River.

# Benton's Jail and Gallows

209 W Main St,
Benton, IL 62812
37.99699, -88.92241

The town of Benton sits in the heart of southern Illinois in what is known as Little Egypt because of the confluence of the Ohio and Mississippi Rivers. Benton is the county seat of Franklin and has a town square with a courthouse in the center. A few blocks to the west is a unique-looking building. From the front it looks like a typical two-story brick house such as you would see in any older midwestern city. As you move around to the side, you see a large brick attachment to the rear about twice the length of the house and two rows of windows. This was the old county jail, and the house was the sheriff's residence, built in 1905.

Over the decades when it was in use, I am sure the cells have held many thieves, murderers, suspects and intoxicated people, but one person stands out among them. Charlie Birger was a local gang leader selling bootleg liquor to local miners. He ran gambling houses and speakeasies for years. He was accused of murdering the mayor of nearby West City. He was found guilty and was sentenced to be hanged. His punishment was carried out on April 19, 1928. A gallows stood next to the jail, and tickets were sold to spectators of the execution. Approximately five thousand people witnessed Birger's hanging, which was the last public execution in Illinois. Before his execution, he said, "They've accused me of a lot of things I was never guilty of, but I was guilty of a lot of things which they never accused me of, so I guess we're about even."

The old jail had become outdated and was condemned by the

state in 1990. The Benton Historical Society took ownership of the old building, and it is now run as a historical museum where visitors can see the old cells and a replica of the gallows where Birger was executed. The society also allows visitors the chance to try and escape from one of the jail cells. If you are into escape rooms, the jail in Benton has to be one of the most interesting and historic ones to experience.

The town also gained notoriety when George Harrison came to visit his sister and became the first Beatle to visit the United States before they became famous in the U.S. Harrison's sister's husband was a mining engineer, and the couple moved to Benton so he could work for a local coal mine.

# Kaskaskia Liberty Bell

302 1st St,
Chester, IL 62233
37.9216, -89.91472

You may have heard the saying "You can't get there from here". That is true of the  small town of Kaskaskia, which sits south of St. Louis near Chester Illinois. It sits west of the Mississippi River and is only accessible by leaving Illinois and driving through the state of Missouri. To look at it on a modern map it seems strange to have the state line for Illinois loop out over the river but when the state was created, that was the original path of the Mississippi River. One other thing of interest is that when the state of Illinois was created in 1818, Kaskaskia served as the state capitol until it moved to Vandalia in 1819.

The French settled the area in the early 1700s and created a missionary for converting the indigenous people of the area to Catholicism. The village was named Kaskaskia after the name of the tribe in the area. In 1741, King Louis XV gave the mission a large bell. It was sent over by ship to New Orleans and then up the Mississippi to the mission. In the 1760s, the French ceded a nearby fort they had constructed to the British after the French and Indian War. On July 4, 1778, American forces led by George Rogers Clark took control of the British fort during the Revolutionary War and rang the bell, and from

then on it was known as the Liberty Bell of the West.

During the flood of 1881, the Mississippi River changed course because of deforestation, and instead of looping around Kaskaskia it cut it off from Illinois, flowing straight across. With many years of flooding and isolation, the town dwindled down in population. The bell that King Louis sent to the town was still there and rang during Independence Day celebrations. In 1848, a chapel was built to house the historic bell. It was at this time that a crack was noticed in the bell. During the flood of 1973, the bell was knocked off its stand, and the crack grew longer. Two decades later the bell was once again washed off its stand in the flood of '93, and again the crack was enlarged. After that it was never rang again for fear of permanently damaging the old bell. It still stands in the chapel in the isolated town of Kaskaskia.

It is now a state historical site. Visitors can see the bell behind gates on the front door. The door has bars in front of it and remains closed to shelter the historic bell. Visitors can push a green button to remotely open the door. A white doorbell button starts an audio recording. When I pushed the button, I thought it was broken because there was a delay when the door opened. It was like a ghost from the past opened the door. It reminded me of the movie Shrek when Donkey pushed the button for singing children,and after it was over he said, "Let's do that again!"

Independence Day ceremonies are still held at the little chapel. Unfortunately, nobody will be able to hear the sound of the Liberty Bell of the West again since it is too fragile to ring.

# Cardinal Point Witness Corner

Intersection of County Road
2400 N. and US-51,
Centralia, IL 62801
38.47414, -89.14398

South of the town of Centralia along US-51 is a roadside park
where it crosses County Road 2400 N. It seems like a small
place with little significance, but in actuality the location was
vital to the establishment of the state of Illinois. In 1785, the
young country realized they needed a way of surveying land

and established a grid system. Principal Meridian lines ran north and south. The first one was established in Ohio, and the second in Indiana. The third Principal Meridian was established in 1815, and ran north and south from the confluence of the Ohio and Mississippi Rivers.

The baseline which establishes an east and west line was surveyed in Indiana and extends through Illinois. The spot where the Third Principal Meridian and the baseline cross is the Cardinal Point and where sixty percent of the state of Illinois was surveyed from. US-51 passed over the point, and it was eventually paved over. Because of the highway, a new marker was established. Known as a Witness Corner, the marker stands in the small roadside park and is used by surveyors. Today motorists pass over the Cardinal Point that established many of the Prairie State's counties and townships, but few know about its significance.

In 1976, the original marker was rediscovered under the roadway, and a removable plate was installed over it. A stone marker commemorating Cardinal Point was placed in the park at the Witness Corner.

# Cholera Cross

11601 Germantown Rd,
Breese, IL 62230
38.59038, -89.5353

I have traveled down many expressways and back roads. I have
seen many roadside crosses. Some are memorials to loved ones
who died in an automobile or motorcycle accident. Between
the towns of Breese and Germantown in southern Illinois in
front of a dairy farm is a twenty-five foot tall cross that stands

as a thank you and harkens back to a dark period in the middle 1800s.

Cholera spread throughout the midwest in the 1830s. At that time, nobody understood how it was transmitted, but it spread quickly and was deadly. In the morning, a person would be perfectly healthy and later that night have a fever. The following day they would be dead. During the height of the pandemic, over six hundred people died of cholera in St Louis. In rural areas, entire families would be wiped out in a matter of weeks.

In 1850, farmer and German emigrant Henry J. Altepeter prayed to God to spare his family. If his family survived, he promised he would erect a cross on his farm in gratitude for his mercy. After the pandemic had swept through the farmland of southern Illinois, Altepeter erected a large wooden cross. The wood decayed and had to be replaced a few times, and was eventually replaced by a white concrete cross. It still stands as a reminder of the difficult times the early pioneers faced and the mercy one family was given.

The German words "Im Kreuz Ist Heil" is written on the cross and translates to English as "In the cross is whole" or "In the cross is Salvation"; I have seen it translated both ways. I am thinking the latter sounds better and is more appropriate given its history.

# Hutson Memorial Cabins

16297 N 1550th St
Hutsonville, IL 62433
39.08956, -87.65751

The town of Hutsonville sits along the Wabash River, which makes up the Illinois and Indiana border. South of town is a group of log buildings that make up the Hutson Memorial Cabins to memorialize Isaac Hutson and his family, for whom the town of Hutsonville was named after.

Isaac Hutson, his wife, and their family of six children came to the area in the winter of 1812. He built a log cabin not far from the current memorial cabins. In April 1813, Isaac took a trip to the fort in Palestine. When he returned, he found his wife and children had been massacred by local Native Americans. His cabin had been set on fire and burned to the ground. Isaac joined the army in Terre Haute and was eventually killed in battle near Fort Harrison by one of the local tribes. A few decades later when the town was platted, they chose the name in honor of the slain family.

In 1967, Wayne Brock offered the Hutsonville Chamber of Commerce a log cabin that was built in 1892. The cabin was disassembled and moved to property south of town. Over time, several other log cabins along with period furniture were donated, and the cabins created a memorial village to remind people of the area's history.

During the summer months, various churches hold services and weddings in the old log cabin church at the village.

# Vandalia State House

315 W Gallatin St,
Vandalia, IL 62471
38.96119, -89.09394

In downtown Vandalia is a large white building with columns at the entrance. It looks as if it has great significance because it did. The building was built in 1836 and served as the fourth capitol building for the state of Illinois. Vandalia became the capital in 1819 after it was moved from Kaskaskia. Two other state houses were constructed before the one that stands today. It served as the capitol for only a few years because it was moved to Springfield in 1839. The second floor held the Senate and House of Representatives chambers. It is where Abraham Lincoln began his political career and was paid $4 a day. Today the Old State Capitol is a museum and welcomes visitors to explore a time when Honest Abe represented the people of Illinois.

On the southwest corner of the state house grounds is a large statue of a woman in pioneer dress holding a baby while her young son embraces her legs. The statue named "Madonna of the Trail" was placed in Vandalia in 1928 by the National Society, Daughters of the American Revolution. They wanted to honor the trails leading across the country and promote public roles for women in the 1920s. Twelve statues were placed across the United States, and the town of Vandalia was chosen because it was the western terminus of the National Road. The road was intended to connect the east coast with the Mississippi River and end at St. Louis. Funds ran out in 1839, and with the popularity of the railroads, the National Road ended in Vandalia. The statue stands not only as a testament to the pioneering women of the western frontier but a reminder of the National Road.

# McPike Mansion

2018 Alby St,
Alton, IL 62002
38.90603, -90.18362

Alton Illinois sits on the other side of the river from St. Louis Missouri and is considered part of the metro St. Louis area. Up on a hill north of town sits an old brick mansion surrounded by large old trees. The home is said to be one of the most haunted houses in America. It was built in 1869 by

Henry McPike. He was a local businessman and politician who served as Alton's mayor for a few years.

The mansion sits on fifteen acres, and McPike grew award-winning grapes for the wine he made in the home's cellar. The family lived in the home until their deaths when the house was sold to Paul A. Laichinger in 1925. He lived in the home while renting rooms to others until his death in 1945. The home sat neglected for decades, and vandals broke in and stole most of the architectural components of the house. It was saved from the wrecking ball when it was sold at auction in 1994 to Sharyn and George Luedke.

The Luedkes began the process of renovating the home and noticed strange occurrences—the sound of voices or whistling or cold spots as people passed through the rooms. They believe it was the spirits of Henry McPike and his family. His daughter was known to participate in whistling competitions and maybe she is still whistling from beyond the grave. The home is privately owned but is open for tours and ghost hunts. You can see more at their website www.Mcpikemansion.com

The mansion has been featured on several television shows, including an episode of the *Travel Channel's Ghost Adventures* and in the series *Ghost Lab.*

# Robert Wadlow Statue

2810 College Ave,
Alton, IL 62002
38.90418, -90.14361

On College Avenue across from the Southern Illinois
University School Dental Medicine is a small park. In the
middle is a statue of a man with a cane that is taller than your
average person or even taller than a professional basketball
player. It is a lifesize statue of Robert Wadlow who is the

*Guiness Book of World Records'* tallest man. He was born in 1918 in Alton. He grew up in the town, and because of a pituitary gland disorder, he grew at an abnormal rate. By the time he was eight years old, he was taller than his father. By the time he entered high school, he was eight feet tall.

1n 1936, he toured with the Ringling Brothers Circus, entertaining folks in the center ring. He was never in the sideshow and preferred to dress in ordinary clothes and refused to wear a costume. He did promotional work for the International Shoe Company which provided him with custom made footwear. He wore leg braces to help with support and while doing an appearance at the Manistee National Forest Festival in Michigan his braces cut into his ankle, leading to an infection. He died on July 15th at the age of 22; at the time he was eight feet and eleven inches tall. He was laid to rest at Oakwood Cemetery in Alton. A life-size statue of Robert stands at the park where visitors can stand next to it to get a feel for how tall he was.

The Alton Museum of History and Art has his custom-made oversized third-grade desk and other artifacts on display.

# Brussels Small Jail

124 Main St,
Brussels, IL 62013
38.94917, -90.58687

The small town of Brussels, Illinois is situated between the Illinois and Mississippi Rivers north of St. Louis. The region was first settled in 1822, and about two decades later several German immigrants moved into the area. St. Mary's Church was formed in the 1840s; the brick church is one of the oldest buildings in town. Down the road from the church is a big white building that serves as the Village Hall. It is an impressive looking building for a small town.

On the main street through town between the church and the hall, next to a bar, is a small building with faded red corrugated metal siding. It looks like it might be a storage shed, but the sign hanging over the door lets people know its historical significance; it reads: **Brussels Village Jail Est. 1876.**

Known locally as the "Calaboose", the little jail was mainly used to hold men who had had too much to drink. It was a place for them to spend the night and the alcohol to work its way out of their bodies. On one occasion, the little jail held twelve men, and if they wanted to "sleep it off" they had to do it standing up. The jail held its last inmate in 1952. After that, they were taken by the sheriff to the county jail.

I think the best way to get to Brussels is to take the car ferry near Grafton across the Illinois River. It feels like an adventure if you have to take a ferry ride to get to your destination. Best of all, the ferry is operated by the Illinois Department of Transportation and is free to use since it is paid for by the taxpayers.

Both Lower Lake, California and Haswell, Colorado jails are said to be the smallest jails in the United States. I have not visited them personally, but looking at the photos they look larger than the jail in Brussels.

# The Old Prison in Alton

218 William St,
Alton, IL 62002
38.89114, -90.1895

The town of Alton sits along the Mississippi River about twenty miles north of St Louis. In the shadow of a giant grain elevator and a parking lot for downtown businesses is a small section of a stone wall. It is all that remains of Illinois' first prison built in 1833. The prison closed in 1857, and the prisoners were transferred to the new prison in Joliet.

During the Civil War, the Union needed more locations to hold Confederate prisoners of war. The military decided to reopen the closed prison in Alton in 1862. The prison could hold up to 1750 prisoners, and during the war over eleven thousand prisoners passed through the penitentiary. Not all were able to leave its walls alive. The old prison was overcrowded and had poor sanitary conditions. Many prisoners died of disease, including three hundred who died from a smallpox epidemic. They were quarantined on an island on the other side of the Mississippi River and their bodies buried after they succumbed to the deadly disease. The island is now covered over by the waters of the Mississippi River. The prison closed after the war and was demolished.

The stones from the former prison were used in the construction of some of the buildings and walls around Alton.

# Cahokia Courthouse

107 Elm St,
Cahokia, IL 62206
38.57092, -90.19205

The village of Cahokia was located south of East St. Louis near the Mississippi River. The village no longer officially exists because it was incorporated into Cahokia Heights due to declining population. Nestled among the trees behind the village offices is a log cabin-style building that is considered to be the oldest building in Illinois.

The building was originally built by the French in 1740. In 1793, it was used as a courthouse for the Northwest Territory. It was in this courthouse that Lewis and Clark planned their expedition while camped nearby during the winter of 1803.

Because of its historical significance, the building was dismantled and moved to St. Louis for the 1904 World's Fair and then two years later to Chicago for the 1906 World's Fair. In 1939, the old courthouse was finally moved back to its original site where it stands today and is maintained by the National Park Service.

The Jarrot Mansion State Historic site stands a few blocks east of the Cahokia Courthouse.

# Fifth District Appellate Court

Main St & N 14th St,
Mt Vernon, IL 62864
38.31754, -88.90838

Illinois Route 15 travels east and west across southern Illinois.
Through downtown Mt Vernon, it splits into two one-way
streets and becomes Main Street heading west. Before it curves

back into a two way road, motorists head straight towards an old white building with a unique arched stairway. Standing in front of the building is a statue of Abrahm Lincoln.

The building is the 5th District Appellate Court built in 1854. Illinois' constitution established five appellate courts, and they are the courts of first appeal for civil and criminal cases rising in the Illinois Circuit Courts. In November 1859, Abraham Lincoln was here on behalf of his client, the Illinois Central Railroad, which was being sued by the State of Illinois to collect taxes for the year 1857. The courthouse has the only remaining courtroom in which Abraham Lincoln tried a case that continues to be used to this day in the same manner it was used in the 1850s.

# Chapter 2
# Central Illinois

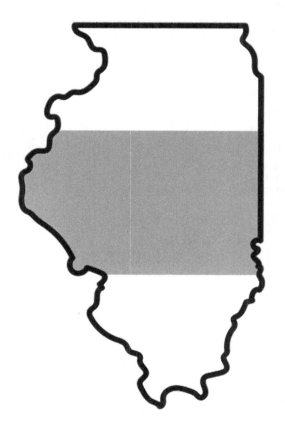

# Annie Louise Keller

Whiteside Park
180 S Main St,
White Hall, IL 62092
39.43591, -90.40336

The small town of White Hall stands southwest of Springfield
in rural Illinois. There you will find Whiteside Park and a stone
monument surrounded by a metal fence. Carved on the top of
the white stone is a woman with her arms around a young boy
and girl.

At first glance, you might think this is a carving of a mother and her children, but looking more closely, the boy is holding a school book. It is a memorial to a teacher who gave her life while protecting her students.

On April 19, 1927, a storm was racing across the Illinois countryside. Annie Louise Keller was the school teacher at Centerville School in White Hall. When she saw the approaching storm, Keller ordered her sixteen pupils under their desks while she stood near the wall at the front door. A tornado ripped through the area and destroyed the school. Townsfolk rushed to the pile of boards and timber that once made up the schoolhouse. Miraculously, they found all of the children alive protected by their school desks. Tragically, they found the body of Annie Louise Keller under the wall she was standing next to. She gave her life protecting the students she taught and loved.

School children from around Illinois raised four thousand dollars, and the state pitched in five thousand for a memorial to the heroic teacher. The monument that stands in White Hall was erected in her honor two years after the horrific tornado.

The monument was carved by Illinois native and renowned sculptor Lorado Taft. Many of his sculptures, including *Lincoln The Lawyer* in Urbana, Illinois, can be seen around the state.

# Inventor of the Dishwasher

148 S. Broadway St.
Shelbyville, IL 62565
39.40591, -88.79373

The town of Shelbyville is south of Decatur in the center of Illinois. An unassuming two-story house sits on Broadway Street behind the downtown shops. A stone marker that looks like a tombstone stands next to the road in front of the old house. It does not mark a death but a new beginning of freedom from housework. It was in the shed behind the house that a modern kitchen appliance was created.

In the 1870s, Josephine Chocrane lived with her husband Wiliiam. He was a dry goods merchant and politician, and the couple lived in the upper class society and had servants to cook and clean for them. She noticed her fine china was being chipped, and frustrated with the hired servants, she washed the dishes herself. She noticed she also chipped a few of the plates and realized the need for a better and easier way to wash the dishes.

She sketched up plans for making her own dishwasher. While she was working on her dishwasher plans, her husband died in 1883. After his death, Josephine learned that her husband was deeply in debt and she was not as wealthy as she had thought. She was in need of income, so she continued to work on her dishwasher, hoping the sale of her invention would provide her with the money that she needed. Josephine got help with making her prototype from local railroad mechanic George Butters. Other people had invented dishwashers, but they used scrubbing brushes for cleaning. Josephine's innovative design uses water pressure to clean dishes without chipping or breaking them.

After building successful machines, she displayed them at the Chicago World's Fair in 1893. At $100 each, they were too expensive for the average housewife. Instead she focused on hotels and restaurants. Eventually, she was able to get the price down to build units for residential use. Her company was eventually sold to KitchenAid, now part of Whirlpool Corporation. A stone marker stands in front of the privately owned house that changed housework for people around the world.

In 2006, Josephine Chocrane was inducted into the National Inventors Hall of Fame.

# Two-Story Outhouse

1022 S Pine St,
Gays, IL 61928
39.45887, -88.49559

Along IL-16 is the small town of Gays. There in Gene Goodwin Park you will find a curious tall white structure. The narrow building is a two-story outhouse and draws laughter and wonder by visitors. It was built in 1872 by Samuel Gammill. He owned a general store in town that had an apartment upstairs.

He built the outhouse with a walkway to it from the upper floor, eliminating the need to go up and down stairs. The holes for the upper and lower floors are opposite each other and separated by a wall so the person using the bottom facility did not see the upper. The old store was demolished in 1984 but the historic outhouse was saved and moved to the park. Visitors can sign a log book, allowing others who visit to know the hometowns of the people who have stopped at the historic outhouse.

# The President's Father

Shiloh Cemetery,
12988 E Lincoln Hwy Rd,
Lerna, IL 62440
39.38808, -88.23645

One of the most visited gravesites in the United States is that of President Abraham Lincoln in Oak Ridge Cemetery in Springfield. About ninety miles to the east standing in the farmland near Lerna is a small brick church. The Shiloh Presbyterian Church was built next to the graveyard in 1881 and a brick facade was added in 1921. It is in the cemetery where you will find the gravesite for Thomas Lincoln the father of the 16th President. Thomas was buried in this cemetery after his death in 1851 at the age of 73. Abraham Lincoln visited his father's grave in 1861 shortly before assuming the Presidency. His step-mother Sarah Bush Lincoln was laid to rest next to her husband after her death in 1869. Lincoln's mother Nancy Hanks Lincoln died when he was a boy and is buried in Pioneer Cemetery in Indiana which is now part of the Lincoln Boyhood National Memorial.

The graveyard started out as the Gordon Graveyard named for John Gordon who donated the land in the 1830s. In 1898 John and Susan Baker donated four acres of land north of the church creating the Shiloh Cemetery. In 1935 the two cemeteries were combined into the Thomas Lincoln Cemetery. On maps and the internet you may find any of the three names listed for the cemetery.

The Lincoln Log Cabin State Historic Site is only a couple of miles to the east of the cemetery.

# Ashmore Estates

22645 E Co Rd 1050 N,
Ashmore, IL 61912
39.52944, -88.05111

A large old brick building stands a few miles outside of the small eastern central Illinois town of Ashmore. The building was once part of the Coles County Poor Farm. Built in 1916, it replaced an older building that was constructed when the poor farm was created in the 1870s. It was a place where destitute people could live. The elderly and mentally or physically disabled people who could not work called the farm home. In the early days of the farm, it was not the nicest of places to live. The residents were referred to as inmates, and a report talked of the horrible living conditions. It claimed the walls were infested with vermin and flies swarmed everywhere, especially at mealtime.

Because of the poor conditions, the current building that is still standing was constructed. It was used by the county until 1959, when it was sold into private ownership to be used as a psychiatric hospital and named Ashmore Estates. The building changed ownership a few times but never became financially feasible, and it closed permanently in the 1980s.

The building sat vacant and was vandalized over the years. It was sold in 1998 for twelve thousand dollars. The new owner wanted to convert it into a private residence but abandoned the project. The old building was then sold again and used as a haunted attraction. A storm in 2013 severely damaged the roof, and it was sold again to the current owner. They have made repairs and renovated much of the outside of the building.

The old poorhouse and psychiatric building is used as a historic and haunted attraction. Visitors can tour the old building, learning of its history while hunting for ghosts. You can learn more about tours on their website www.ashmoreestates.net.

Ashmore Estates was featured on the *Travel Channel's Ghost Adventures* and *Destination Fear* along with *Syfy's Ghost Hunters*.

# Chesterville Cemetery Witch

Chesterville Cemetery
371 N Co Rd 450 E,
Arthur, IL 61911
39.70599, -88.3865

The shadow town of Chesterville sits near Arcola in the heart of Amish country. Near the Kaskaskia River you will find the Chesterville Cemetery. Legend has it the old cemetery is where a young witch was buried. A large oak tree grows over a gravesite and marks the location of the grave.

The story goes that over a century ago a teenage girl rebelled against her Amish upbringing and spoke out against the treatment of women in her community. Because she had the audacity to question her religion, she was shunned by the community and deemed a witch. The young woman went missing, and then her body was discovered in a field; the cause of her death was unknown.

Her body was laid to rest in the town cemetery, and an iron fence was placed around the grave. An oak tree was planted over her grave to keep her spirit from escaping. Over the decades, the tree grew and has now grown over the fence.

Exactly how true the story is, I am not sure, but it is interesting to see how the tree has consumed the fence. I prefer not to think of it as a tale of sadness but one of hope that as we pass on our spirit and story continues to grow and spread like the tree over the gravesite. I have visited a lot of gravesites in my travels, but I was moved by the enormous size and beauty of the oak tree. I must not be the only one who has visited the gravesite since there had been several artificial flowers placed on the fence and her grave.

A wooden sign with the words Frauke Yoder has been added to the fence. The German translation for *frauke* means "little girl" in English. Yoder is a common surname in Amish Country.

# Prairie Observatory

Walnut Point State Park
2331 East CR 370 N,
Oakland, IL 61943
39.70178, -88.05359

Deep within the Walnut Point State Park near Oakland is an old abandoned building with a large dome on the roof. It was the Prairie Observatory constructed in 1969 by the University of Illinois at Urbana-Champaign's Department of Astronomy. The site was chosen because of the minimal amount of man-made light, providing for a dark sky. The observatory had a forty-inch telescope that cost about a quarter of a million dollars. In 1981, the telescope was moved to San Diego State University's Mount Laguna Observatory where it is still being utilized. The building was abandoned and sits mostly forgotten.

The interior of the building is off limits to the public, and the main entrance has been sealed off by concrete blocks. Hikers can still see the outside as it is slowly being engulfed by the surrounding trees and vegetation. It can be viewed from trails that start in Walnut Point State Park or from N. Co. Rd. 2200 E. When I visited, the gate was open from the county road, allowing access to a parking area; it was about a two hundred yard hike to the old observatory. There was a note about hunting, so I think they closed the gate during hunting season.

The three-mile long Observatory Trail takes hikers past the old abandoned observatory. It is in a low area of the park and is prone to flooding and can get muddy during times of rain.

# The POWs of Greenwood Cemetery

606 S Church St,
Decatur, IL 62522
39.83372, -88.95606

Greenwood Cemetery sits on the south side of Decatur. It was started in the early 1800s and has old and ornate tombstones and mausoleums of Ilinoisans who were laid to rest decades ago. The cemetery also has a large Civil War veterans section.

Tombstones of Union Soldiers encompass a monument in their honor.

There are reports that claim a large number of confederate soldiers were buried in the cemetery in unmarked mass graves. During the Civil War, trains transporting Confederate prisoners of war to Union prison camps would pass through Decatur. One of the trains was stricken by yellow fever, and many of the soldiers died on the train. It is said that the train tracks passed near Greenwood Cemetery. The locomotive stopped, and the bodies of the dead southern soldiers were buried in mass graves at the edge of the cemetery. Some claim to have seen the ghosts of the soldiers roaming the cemetery. The cemetery is said to be one of the most haunted in Illinois. I am not sure about that, but it is a beautiful and interesting old cemetery with a lot of history.

# St. Omer Witch

End of St Omer Rd,
Ashmore, IL 61912
39.56855, -88.03095

Surrounded by the farm fields north of Ashmore is the old St. Omer Cemetery. It is all that remains of the town of St. Omer. It has many old tombstones, but one stands out among them. It is a stone sphere atop a pedestal carved out of stone to look like logs. It is the grave marker for Marcus Barnes, his parents

77

Granville and Sarah, and his wife, Caroline.

It is Caroline's name and dates that make people wonder about her death. Carved into the sphere, it reads that she died on February 31, 1882. Legend has it that she was a witch or was accused of being one. The story claims the sphere used as her tombstone was a crystal ball which is said to glow on moonless nights. It was believed that the witch would rise on the anniversary of her death, and to prevent that from happening, the date of February 31 was carved into her marker, knowing that date would never come.

Most likely the date was a typo that was never corrected because there were no living relatives to care about the error, and over the years the story grew around the mistake.

# Lincoln Colored Home

427 S 12th St,
Springfield, IL 62703
39.79756, -89.63976

The city of Springfield serves as the Illinois State Capitol. The city has several historically significant homes and buildings, including Abraham Lincoln's residence while he lived in the city. A few blocks east of the Lincoln House on 12th Street is an old two-story brick structure. It is in a dilapidated state with the windows boarded up and a chain link fence surrounding it to keep out vandals.

The building may not be much to look at, but it was important in our nation's history. It was known as the Lincoln Colored Home and was the first orphanage for African American children. In the late 1800s, Springfield had three orphanages, but African American children were not allowed. In 1898, Eva Carroll Monroe put one hundred twenty-five dollars on an old house on 12th Street to create her orphanage. Most of the citizens of Springfield thought Monroe was foolish in trying to start her orphanage, but she became friends with Mary Lawrence, the widow of former Springfield mayor, Rheuna Lawrence. With Lawrence's financial help and political connections, Monroe was able to build a new building for her orphanage in 1904. It replaced the original home and stands today. The orphanage had architectural pieces such as stained glass windows and a chandelier from Lawrence's home after it was remodeled under the supervision of renowned architect Frank Lloyd Wright.

The orphanage closed in 1933 after the foster system replaced the use of orphanages. Today the historic structure is privately owned, and the current owners hope to one day restore it. Although it may be in a rough and deteriorated condition, it still stands as a reminder of a time when African American orphaned children were given a place to live when the nation ignored them.

# Purple Martin Capital

201-257 W Quincy St,
Griggsville, IL 62340
39.70824, -90.72674

The town of Griggsville sits in the eastern central part of Illinois between the Illinois and Mississippi Rivers. In the center of town is a strange looking tower, and from a distance it looks like some sort of antenna covered in white boxes. It is actually covered in man-made birdhouses for purple martins. Part of the swallow family, purple martins feed on flying insects and can eat up to two thousand mosquitoes a day.

Purple Martins are extremely adept at flying and eating insects. Unfortunately, they are not good at building nests, and at one time were almost extinct. In the 1960s, Griggsville resident J. L. Wade manufactured television antennas. He was a nature lover and  began mounting birdhouses to antennas to attract the purple martins and help control mosquitos and limit the use of pesticides. A seventy foot tower was erected in the center of town and holds birdhouses for five hundred sixty birds. The town proclaimed it is the Purple Martin Capital of the nation.

# Trail of Death Marker

308 Park St,
Liberty, IL 62347
39.87951, -91.10675

Illinois Route 104 travels east and west from Taylorville to Quincy. About twenty miles to the east of Quincy is the small town of Liberty, where Route 104 makes up Main Street. A block off Main Street to the east is a small park with a boulder that marks the Trail of Death.

On September 4, 1838, approximately 860 members of the Potawatomi nation were forcibly removed from northern Indiana. Their village was burned down, and all of the men, women and children were marched over six hundred miles to Nebraska by one hundred armed militia soldiers. Along the way, over 40 people died; 28 of them were children. On the 33rd day of the 60-day march, they stopped to camp near present day Liberty. A boulder with a plaque sits in the park to remember the march known as the Trail of Death.

In the 1990s, the Trail of Death was declared a Regional Historic Trail by the state legislatures of Indiana, Illinois, Kansas and Missouri. 74 markers have been placed along the route, including the one in Liberty.

There is another rock in the park that is said to have mystical powers. The rock was supposedly found in a farmer's field over fifty years ago, dragged to the park and put on display. It is an oddly shaped rock that to me looks like the tip of a male private part. It is known as "the baby making rock" and legend claims that if a woman sits on it that it will increase her fertility and she will get pregnant. I am thinking the legend comes from the shape of the rock, but this is only a guess.

# Newcomb-Stillwell Mansion

1601 Maine St,
Quincy, IL 62301
39.93226, -91.38982

On the corner of 16th and Main in the city of Quincy stands a
three-story mansion that looks like a castle. The Richardson
Romanesque style house is made of stone quarried near
Cleveland Ohio. It was built in 1891 by Richard Newcomb to

impress the citizens of Quincy, which it most definitely did, and it is still impressive to this present day.

Newcomb was the founder of the Quincy Paper Company. After Richard Newcomb's death, his daughter and son-in-law John A. Stillwell moved into the massive home in the 1920s. After the Stillwells died in the 1930s, the house was given over to Quincy College and named Stillwell Hall. It was used as a dormitory. During World War II, it was used as a headquarters for the Red Cross and a dormitory for participants in the Civilian Pilot's Training Program. In the 1980s, the college sold the house to Quincey Museum Inc. After a million dollar renovation, the first floor of the house was renovated to the way it was when it was first constructed. The upper floor displays museum exhibits.

The city of Quincy has several other historic homes, including John Wood Mansion and the William S. Warfield House.

# Cattle Bank

102 E University Ave,
Champaign, IL 61820
40.11645, -88.2386

Near downtown Champaign on the corner of 1st and University Drive is an old brick building, and at one time it was adorned with the words "Cattle Bank" on the sides. In the mid-1800s, the city was the southern end of the rail line heading into Chicago. Ranchers drove their cattle to

Champaign to be shipped by rail cars to the slaughter houses in Chicago. The bank was built in 1858 and provided ranchers and cattlemen with financial services. The bank was only in operation for three years, but it is believed that Abraham Lincoln cashed a check at the bank.

After the bank closed in 1861, the building was used as a grocery store. In 1971, a fire destroyed most of the interior, and it was slated to be demolished. Citizens stepped in to renovate the historic building. It now serves as the Champaign County History Museum and is the oldest building in the city.

# Carthage Jail

 305 Walnut St,
Carthage, IL 62321
40.41521, -91.13933

In the town of Carthage, a block south of US-136 is a two-story building. It has large reddish colored stones and white framed windows. It was built in 1839 and was the county jail until 1866. It was in this building in 1844 that Joseph Smith and his Brother Hyrum were killed. Joseph was the founder of the Latter-Day Saints Movement and had moved his followers to Nauvoo along the Mississippi River about thirty miles from Carthage.

Concerns about his polygamy began to grow around eastern Illinois and western Missouri. Joseph Smith ordered his followers to destroy the printing press used by the Nauvoo Expositor for printing negative stories about him. After Governor Ford's threat of sending the militia to quell the violence, Joseph and his brother surrendered to the jail in Carthage. Two days later, an armed mob stormed the jail and shot Hyrum in the face as he tried to block the door. Joseph

Smith fired three shots from a pepper-box pistol that his friend, Cyrus Wheelock, had lent him, wounding three men. Smith was shot several times as he jumped out the window and fell to the ground, where he was shot several more times by the crowd, ending his life. Today the jail is owned by the Church of Jesus Christ of Latter-day Saints and has been restored to the way it was in 1844.

The nearby city of Nauvoo contains the Nauvoo Historic District and is a National Historic Landmark District. In the 1950s, Mormon preservationists purchased and restored Mormon sites, including Bringham Young's home and Joseph Smith's homestead.

# Mother Jones

Union Miners Cemetery
5535 Mt Olive Rd,
Mt Olive, IL 62069
39.08068, -89.73334

Mount Olive is about fifty miles south of Springfield. It is where you will find the Union Miners Cemetery. There you will see a large stone monument flanked by the statues of miners holding a pickaxe and a sledgehammer. The monument is for Mary G. Harris Jones also known as "Mother Jones."

Mary was born sometime in the 1830s in Ireland. Her exact birth date has been lost to history. Because of the Great Potato Famine, she emigrated to Canada when she was a teenager and studied to become a teacher. In 1861, she moved to Memphis, Tennessee and married George E. Jones, a member and organizer of the National Union of Iron Moulders. Six years later, her husband and their four children died of yellow fever.

Distraught from the death of her family, she moved to Chicago and opened a dressmaking shop. A few years later, the Great Fire of 1871 destroyed her shop and home. It was during the rebuilding of Chicago that Mary Jones became active in the labor movement and helped in organizing strikes for fair wages. She believed a man should make enough money that his wife could stay home and raise their children. I know that statement is sexist in today's standards, but it was a big leap forward back then.

Mary became a member of the United Mine Workers and helped organize strikes across the nation. She was arrested several times, and in one court case in West Virginia, an attorney representing a mining company claimed she was "the most dangerous woman in America". At the age of 60, she took on the persona of Mother Jones and fought for the rights of poor working Americans. In 1903, Jones organized children who were working in mills and mines to participate in her famous "March of the Mill Children", where they marched from Pennsylvania to President Theodore Roosevelt's summer home on Long Island.

Mother Jones was a prolific and influential speaker and worked with the unions into her 90s. She died on November 30, 1930 at her friend's home in Silver Springs, Maryland. She was laid to rest in the Union Miners Cemetery in Mount Olive near the miners who died in the 1898 Battle of Virden, a riot that occurred as part of a union strike.

Mother Jones' achievements were never recognized like women of the Suffrage Movement and when asked about this, she said, "You don't need to vote to raise hell." In 1984, she was inducted into the National Women's Hall of Fame.

# Forgottonia

Train Station in Macomb
120 E Calhoun St,
Macomb, IL 61455
40.46137, -90.67098

The city of Macomb sits in the farmland of central western Illinois. Above the train depot is a sign for "Unforgettable Forgottonia". The region that sits between the Mississippi and Illinois Rivers is sparsely populated, and during the 70s there were only six bridges that crossed the Illinois River into the fourteen-county area. Being somewhat isolated from the rest of the Land of Lincoln and having their rail services cut, some prominent citizens adopted the name The Republic of Forgottonia.

The region got some notoriety from reporters as the group threatened to succeed from Illinois and form their own state. Obviously, they never created a fifty-first state, but it did help in bringing new train routes and roads through the region. Although the movement may have slowed down since the 1970s, the sign still hangs from the eve at the train station in Macomb and you can see references to Forgottonia in other places around the area, most notably the Forgottonia Brewery in Macomb.

# Camp Ellis

Rifle Range Road
Table Grove, IL
40.38831, -90.35047

Easley Pioneer Museum
210 W Broadway St,
Ipava, IL 61441

The small town of Ipava lies about forty miles southwest of
Peoria. In the 1940s, it had a population of about six hundred
people. During World War II, the area north of Ipava was
chosen for a military training base because it was in close
proximity to the railyard in Galesburg and a large relatively flat
section of the state.

The military forced farmers into selling their land and acquired almost 18,000 acres of land to create Camp Ellis, named for Sergeant Michael B. Ellis, a World War I Medal of Honor recipient from East Saint Louis, Illinois. The base was constructed in two months and had over two thousand buildings, including libraries, gymnasiums, seven chapels, an outdoor amphitheater, and a baseball diamond. The base housed over 25,000 troops, and almost overnight it rivaled many of Illinois's largest cities in population. The base trained thousands of soldiers in engineering, medical, maintenance and support jobs. Besides training US soldiers, the base also had a separate section that held five thousand German prisoners of war.

At the end of the war, the base was deemed surplus. Part of it was used by the Illinois National Guard, but they too abandoned the base in the 1950s. The land was converted back into farmland, and today most people driving through the area would not know that it had once been one of the largest military bases in the United States. All that remains are a few foundations and the old rifle range walls. They stand along Rifle Range Road and are covered in graffiti.

> The Easly Pioneer Museum in Ipava has artifacts from Camp Ellis and reminds visitors of the former military base. The museum is open from April to November.

# The Little Girl of Evergreen Cemetery

302 E Miller St,
Bloomington, IL 61701
40.46946, -88.98712

In the back of the historic Evergreen Memorial Cemetery in Bloomington is an old tree stump that has been carved into a girl with a dog. Anyone who has seen the movie or read the book The Wizard of Oz will recognize the girl as the main character of Dorothy. Near the carving is a grave marker for Dorothy Louise Gage, who was the niece of L. Frank Baum, the author of the beloved children's book.

Dorothy was born on Saturday, June 11, 1898 in Bloomington, Illinois to Baum's wife's sister Sophie (Jewell) Gage and her brother-in-law Thomas Clarkson Gage. Five months later, on November 11th, she died of "Congestion of the brain" and was laid to rest in the cemetery. To honor the baby's memory, Baum chose the name Dorothy for the title character in the new book he was writing.

Actor Mickey Carroll played one of the Munchkins in 1939, and his family owned a tombstone business in St. Louis for over sixty years. He donated a new tombstone and placed it next to the original simple gravel marker that had been weathered over the years and became difficult to read. By 2018, the oak tree that overlooked Dorothy's grave had died and the trunk was carved into the statue that stands as a reminder of a baby girl who was immortalized by her uncle. If you visit, you can find Dorothy's marker about five rows back and two to the right of the carving. It has a small bush on both sides of it.

Illinois Governor and presidential candidate Adlai Stevenson was raised in Bloomington and laid to rest in Evergreen Memorial Cemetery.

# The House in Watseka

 300 E Sheridan St,
Watseka, IL 60970
40.78329, -87.7306

At the north end of Watseka stands a large brick two-story home. It looks like an ordinary midwestern house, but a story from its past makes people wonder what secrets the walls contain.

In 1877, Mary Lurancy Vennum was born near the town of Watseka. At the age of thirteen, she had trouble sleeping at night, telling her family that she heard voices calling to her. She started having seizures and psychotic episodes, claiming to be possessed by someone else's spirit. Her relatives told the family to have her admitted to an asylum for treatment. Instead, her parents took her to see E. W. Stevens, a local renowned spiritualist.

According to Stevens, Vennum's body was taken over by other spirits. She spoke in different voices and became several different people, including an old woman named Katrina Hogan and a young man named Willie Canning. Eventually, she became possessed by the spirit of Mary Roff, who had died twelve years earlier. Mary Roff's parents lived in the home that stands on the north side of town and after meeting with Vennum, they were convinced she was possessed by their daughter's spirit. They invited Vennum to live with them, and after staying at the Roff home for several weeks, Mary's spirit eventually left and Vennum returned to her normal self. She later married and moved to California, living a long life. E. W. Stevens wrote a book titled *The Watseka Wonder* about the ordeal.

C. W. Raymond came to own the house after the Roffs. He served as a federal judge in the Oklahoma territory, and after his death in 1939, Raymond's step-daughter Katharine Clifton inherited the house. She owned several farms in the region and built a runway behind the house so she could fly an airplane around to view the status of the crops.

Currently the home is owned by John Whitman, who restored it to its original condition. It is used for private events and rented to guests on Airbnb.

# Chapter 3
# Northern Illinois

# Statue of the Republic

Near 6401 S Richards Dr,
Chicago, IL 60649
41.7796, -87.57992

A statue of a woman gilded in gold holding a globe in one hand and a staff in the other stands at the intersection of E. Hayes Dr. and S. Richards Dr. in Jackson Park. It is a replica of the sixty- five-foot tall Statue of the Republic that stood in the 1893 World's Columbian Exposition, also known as the

Chicago World's Fair. It celebrated the 400th anniversary of Columbus "discovering" America.

Jackson Park was the grounds of the exposition and had two hundred buildings that were constructed for the fair. Their facades were covered in a white plaster-like substance to create ornate looking architectural styles. They were built to be temporary structures, and because of the white plaster they were nicknamed the "White City". The exposition showcased the technological advances and industrial wonders at the end of the 19th century. It was the location of the first Ferris Wheel and where Pabst got its blue ribbon for his beer. Over twenty-seven million people visited the fair from May to October in the summer of 1893.

Most of the buildings of the exposition were designed to be temporary structures. While some were being dismantled, many Chicagoans petitioned to have them remain standing in Jackson Park. A fire in 1894 that raced through the White City dashed any hopes of saving most of the buildings for future generations. The only two remaining structures are the Art Institute of Chicago, which was the World's Congress Auxiliary Building, and the Museum of Science and Industry, which was the Palace of Fine Arts.

The Statue of the Republic was designed by Daniel Chester French, who also designed the statue of Abraham Lincoln at the Lincoln Memorial in Washington D.C. After the exposition, the massive statue was ordered to be destroyed by fire. I don't understand how they could have purposely eradicated such a beautiful work of art. In 1918, a smaller scale replica was erected for the 25th anniversary of the World's Columbian Exposition.

One of the ticket booths was converted into a garden shed at the DeCaro home on Forest Ave in Oak Park.

# Joliet Prison

401 Woodruff Rd,
Joliet, IL 60432
41.54569, -88.07184

The town of Joliet is located a few miles north of Interstate 80 where the former Joliet Correctional Center stands. The old prison is where Elwood picked up his brother Jake in *The Blues Brothers* movie.

The prison was first constructed in 1858, using blocks quarried from the site by inmates transferred from other prisons. In the early years, not only did it hold criminals but also Confederate Prisoners of War during the Civil War. By 1872, the population had reached 1,239, a record number for a single prison. In the 1930s, Lester Joseph Gillis, better known as Baby Face Nelson, was sentenced to Joliet for 1 to 10 years for bank robbery. He did not stay there long because he escaped while being transferred back to Joliet on another trial.

In the 1960s, prison inmates were used for hepatitis experiments by Willowbrook State School. The military recruited "volunteers" who were draft dodgers sentenced to Joliet during the Vietnam War. The men drank feces-laden chocolate milkshakes and were exposed to the feces of other inmates in an effort to mass-produce and isolate the virus that caused Hepatitis A.

Originally, women were in a separate cell block in the main prison. In 1896, a separate prison modeled to resemble the original one, but with fewer cells, was constructed across the street to hold female inmates. The prison closed in 2002, and is now part of the Joliet Area Historical Museum, and visitors can tour the historic penitentiary. The exterior walls of the old penitentiary look rather ominous and foreboding. I can't imagine what it would have been like to be an inmate.

The prison has been used as a filming location for many TV shows and movies. It was used for the first season of Fox Network's *Prison Break* television show, and the movie *Let's Go to Prison*.

# Norma Jean
# The Circus Elephant

603 5th St,
Oquawka, IL 61469
40.93884, -90.94954

The town of Oquawka sits along the Mississippi River. In the center of town under the shadow of the water tower is a park. Next to a pine tree is a stone monument with an elephant mounted to the top. It stands in memory of a tragic day in the town's history.

The Clark and Walters Circus came to town in the summer of 1972 and had two shows planned for the citizens of Oquawka on July 17. The star of the circus was a 29 year-old elephant named Norma Jean. On the day of the show, a storm blew in and Norma Jean's caretaker, Possum Red, tied her to a tree with a metal chain.

Lighting struck the tree and the electrical charge traveled through the chain and instantly killed Norma Jean. She weighed 6500 pounds and would be difficult to move. It was decided to bury her where she lay. Bulldozers were brought in and dug a pit, and the elephant was laid to rest for all eternity in Oquawka's Park.

A few years later, local pharmacist Wade Meloan raised money to build the memorial that now stands, reminding visitors of the park about Norma Jean the circus elephant.

In 2022, the town of Oquawka honored the memory of Norma Jean and the 50th anniversary of her death with a festival in her honor.

# The Old Ammo Plant

Midewin Iron Bridge Trailhead
Schweitzer Ed Road and IL-53
Elwood, IL 60421
41.379, -88.12318
Old Bunkers located at
41.37513, -88.11889

The Midewin National Tallgrass Prairie lies south of the town of Elwood. In some areas, hikers can see concrete bunkers embedded in the landscape. They are remnants of the land's previous use. At the start of World War II, the U.S. Government decided it would need more arsenal capabilities. In the 1940s, the Army purchased over 450 farms in the area south of Elwood, creating the Joliet Ammunition Plant.

It was at the plant that one of the worst industrial accidents occurred. An explosion in the early morning of June 5, 1942 killed 42 workers. I found conflicting information, but it was either an explosion on an assembly line or workers loading train cars that rocked the northeastern part of Illinois. The blast was equivalent to 62,000 pounds of TNT and shattered windows over four miles away. The explosion was heard by Illinoisans who lived in Waukegan one hundred miles away.

The plant was repaired after the explosion and was used for World War II, the Korean War, and the Vietnam War. It was used for a short period in the 80s and was eventually deactivated in the 90s. The land was reclaimed for public use, and a large part of it became the Midewin National Tallgrass Prairie. The Abraham Lincoln National Cemetery was established on the former ammunition plant grounds, and a monument to the workers killed in the explosion was erected in the cemetery.

During the Civil War in July 1862, President Lincoln signed a law authorizing the establishment of national cemeteries for military veterans, and the cemetery in Elwood was named in honor of the 16th president.

# Rock Island

Rock Island Arsenal Visitor
Welcome Center
23 Prospect Dr, Moline, IL 61265
41.51383, -90.51922

Rock Island is situated in the Mississippi River between Davenport, Iowa and Rock Island, Illinois. In 1816, the government built Fort Armstrong on the island and began manufacturing weapons in the 1880s. The island is home to the largest government weapons manufacturing facility. The Arsenal is the only active U.S. Army foundry, and manufactures

113

ordinance and equipment, including artillery, gun mounts, recoil mechanisms, small arms, aircraft weapons sub-systems, grenade launchers, and weapons simulators.

Along with the manufacturing facilities, the island has many historical sites. The Rock Island National Cemetery is located on the east side of the island. The cemetery also includes a Confederate section for the Prisoner of War soldiers who died in the prison during the Civil War. The Rock Island Arsenal Museum houses an impressive display of military weapons used over the decades. An outside display showcases many historic and experimental cannons and tanks, including Atomic Annie, a cannon that could fire a nuclear shell a distance of five miles.

Near the Mississippi River is Building 301, most commonly called Quarters One. Construction started in 1870 on the Italianate style building. It took almost two years to complete the almost twenty-two thousand square foot house with fifty-one rooms. The house is the second largest home built by the federal government. Only the White House is larger.

It was used as the residence for the commander of Rock Island and had rooms for formal functions and events. Dignitaries such as Charles Lindbergh and King Carl XVI Gustav and Queen Silvia of Sweden have stayed at Quarters One. In 2006, the army discontinued using it as a residence.

Rock Island Arsenal is still an active military base. It does allow civilian visitors, but they have to stop at the visitor center and fill out paperwork and have a background check before a visitor pass is issued.

# John Deere's Blacksmith Shop

8334 S Clinton St,
Dixon, IL 61021
41.8961, -89.41528

Many tractors working in farm fields are green with yellow wheels. They are John Deere tractors, and not only are some of them massive machines, but the company is an enormous global corporation. It is hard to believe that it all started with one man and a blacksmith shop in northern Illinois.

John Deere came to Grand Detour from Vermont in 1836. He built a home for his family and a blacksmith shop where he built cast iron plows. They were the same plows he made to work in the sandy Vermont soil. He quickly realized that the cast iron plows did not work well in the thick rich soil in Illinois that stuck to the plow. He came up with the idea of making polished steel plows that cut through the earth without it sticking to the plow. The sales of his new plow grew over the years and into the company that still bears his name today.

John Deere's home and a replica of his blacksmith shop are now run as an historic site by the John Deere  Corporation.

Visitors can tour the site for free and see blacksmiths working metal just like John Deere did in the 1830s.

> The U.S. National Register of Historic Places was established in 1966. The John Deere House and Shop was one of the first properties to be added to the list. It was added on October 15, 1966, the same day the National Register was established.

# The President's Widow and the Batavia Institute

333 S Jefferson St,
Batavia, IL 60510
41.84458, -88.31646

A few blocks from the Fox River in Batavia is a historic stone building. It was originally built as The Batavia Institute in 1853 by a group of local Congregationalists to be a secondary school because there were few high schools for students to attend in the area at that time. As more public high schools were created in the surrounding towns, it was later granted a charter by the State of Illinois to become a normal school, a school that trains teachers. The Batavia Institute was the second normal school west of the Appalachian Mountains.

The Batavia Institute closed in 1867. The building was then purchased by Dr. Richard J. Patterson, who turned it into a sanitarium for women with mental illnesses, and the name was changed to Bellevue Place. It's most notable resident was Mary Todd Lincoln, the widow of President Abraham Lincoln.

Ten years after the assassination of Abraham Lincoln, their son Robert Todd Lincoln became concerned about his mother's unusual behavior. She was declared insane by a

Chicago court after hearing testimony from seventeen witnesses. She was ordered to be committed to a state mental institution but was permitted to stay at Bellevue Place under Dr. Patterson's care.

The sanitarium was an upscale place that allowed patients to live in a home-like setting. Mrs. Lincoln was permitted to roam the grounds freely and often visited nearby homes. Robert Todd Lincoln would travel by train from Chicago to visit. A few months after entering Bellevue, she gained her freedom and was declared to be sane in court with the help of lawyers James and Myra Bradwell. Myra was one of the earliest female lawyers and helped her case by publicizing Mrs. Lincoln's plight in newspapers. Mary Todd Lincoln went to live with her sister Elizabeth in Springfield.

Eventually, Bellevue Place closed and the building changed hands several times. In the 1960s, it was used as a home for unwed mothers and teenage girls. In the 1980s, the historic building was given a massive renovation, converted into apartments and given the name Bellevue Place. It remains a private apartment complex and is closed to the public. The furniture that Mary Todd Lincoln used when she was a resident can be seen at the Batavia Depot Museum.

Normal School was the name given to schools that instructed teachers in teaching standards and norms. The first normal school west of the Appalacians was Michigan State Normal School, which is now Eastern Michigan University.

# Pullman

610 E 111th St,
Chicago, IL 60628
41.69433, -87.60869

About twelve miles south of downtown Chicago is the town of Pullman, named for the company that created it. In the 1860s, George Pullman developed a passenger car that converted into sleeping berths for passengers to sleep more comfortably. He came up with the concept after sleeping in passenger seats on a long rail journey. The Pullman Company grew into one of the largest railroad car manufactures and employed nearly twenty thousand porters and conductors. To manufacture passenger railcars, the company purchased several acres of swampland south of Chicago near Lake Calumet in the 1880s. The location was ideal because ships could bring in supplies and the nearby rail lines could haul away the completed rail cars.

To attract workers, the company built a town consisting of above average housing. Houses had electricity and running water with indoor toilets, something that many houses at the time did not have. They also built a hotel and public places for workers and their families. The company was thriving at its new Chicago facilities until the recession of 1894. The workers went on strike after the company lowered the workers' wages but did not lower the rent on their housing. The strike was one of the more significant strikes in American history. The American Railroad Union refused to pull trains with Pullman cars, which stopped nearly all rail traffic. The federal government intervened and sent in the army to break up the strike.

The company continued manufacturing rail cars at the Pullman site until 1955, when it closed when the need for passenger rail cars declined due to the rise of the automobile and the interstate highway system. Much of the factory is gone, but the main building with the clock tower remains along with many of the houses once owned by the company. In 2015, the area was designated the Pullman National Historical Park, and the main building has been renovated into a visitors center.

# Shustek Pond

Sign near 7075 Veterans Blvd,
Burr Ridge, IL 60527
41.76104, -87.91815

Shustek Pond lies between County Line Road and an office complex in Burr Ridge southwest of Chicago. The pond is named for a heroic pilot who gave his life to save another. Adventurous twenty-year-old Mary Fahrney wanted to try parachute jumping in July of 1930. Her chute got tangled up in the wing of a plane she was jumping from. After dangling from the plane for an hour, Bruno F. Shustek, a former German pilot in World War 1, jumped from another plane to untangle Fahrney, saving her life. Unfortunately, Shustek lost his grip on the plane and fell to his death.The pond where he landed was officially named Shustek Pond by the United States Board on Geographic Names on April 9, 2015.

# The Beginning of the Nuclear Age

# Paw Paw Woods Nature Preserve
9102 Archer Ave,
Willow Springs, IL 60480
41.70232, -87.91216

A stone monument that looks like a large tombstone stands in the Red Gate Woods located southwest of downtown Chicago. It stands on a hill along a hiking trail, and although it does not mark the location of the buried remains of a person, it does mark something of great significance below the surface.

Most people associate the beginning of the atomic age with the Manhattan Project and Los Alamos, New Mexico. The very first Nuclear Reactor was built in 1942 by a team at the University of Chicago led by physicist Enrico Fermi. The reactor, known as "Chicago Pile 1", was built on a squash court under the bleachers of the abandoned Alonzo Stagg football field. Originally, the first reactor was to be fabricated at a facility in Red Gate Woods, but labor issues delayed construction of the building. The first reactor was mainly a proof of concept and was quickly stopped and disassembled.

A new reactor called Chicago Pile 2 (CP-2) was built in the completed facility dubbed Site A in Red Gate Woods. The new reactor had over 500 tons of uranium and graphite at its core and was shielded by six inches of lead. A third reactor CP-3 was built at Site A and was the first water cooled reactor using plutonium. The reactors did not produce materials for nuclear weapons but were used for research in gaining knowledge of nuclear reactors. CP-2 and CP-3 paved the way for using nuclear reactors in power plants and submarines.

Site A was deactivated in 1954, and the radioactive materials were removed and buried in a nearby location called "Plot M". The buildings were demolished, and the remainder of the reactor was covered over. Beginning in the 1980s, local governments and residents began pressuring the federal government to clean up the former Site A and remove any contaminated soil. In the 1990s, over 500 cubic yards of low-level radioactive soil and debris were removed from the site. After testing by the Illinois Department of Public Health, the site was deemed safe and open to the public for recreational use. A stone cube marks the spot of Plot M, warning to not dig below the surface. Another stone was placed over the buried reactors, marking their location.

# Showmen's Rest

Woodlawn Funeral Home &
Memorial Park
7750 Cermak Rd,
Forest Park, IL 60130
41.85073, -87.8181

Woodlawn Cemetery sits near the Des Plaines River in Forest
Park. There you will find a section that is surrounded by five
statues of elephants. They have their foot on a ball and their
trunks hanging down, which is symbolic of mourning.
Chiseled underneath the elephants are the words "Showmen's
Rest" and "Showmen's League of America". The League was

formed in 1913 with Buffalo Bill Cody as its first president. They purchased 750 plots in Woodlawn Cemetery for a final resting place for circus performers and workers. A few months after Showmen's Rest was created, one of the worst circus train accidents happened nearby.

The town of Hammond, Indiana sits on the border between Indiana and Illinois a few miles south of Lake Michigan. Trains passed through the area on their way around the southern tip of Lake Michigan. It was near Hammond in the summer of 1918 that tragedy struck one of the largest circuses in the country.

At the turn of the century, before movies and television, the circus was a major form of entertainment. They could be massive productions with hundreds of people from performers to laborers to put on a massive traveling show. The Hagenbeck-Wallace Circus was one of the largest in the nation and had an old train and railroad cars to transport its people and animals.

When passing through Hammond, the train stopped to check on some railroad cars for mechanical issues. Signals were set along the tracks to notify approaching locomotives of the stopped train up ahead. An empty transport train hauling passenger cars came into Hammond. The engineer had been operating the locomotive for nearly twenty-four hours and had fallen asleep and missed the signals. It slammed into the back of the circus train. Eighty-six people died, and another one hundred twenty-seven were injured. The wooden railroad cars were ignited by the lanterns and burned after the collision. Many of the bodies of the victims were unrecognizable. The victims of the train wreck were laid to rest in the cemetery, and many of the unidentified graves were simply marked "Unknown Male" or "Unknown Female".

# Ghost church

826 W 19th St,
Chicago, IL 60608
41.85697, -87.64797

The neighborhood of Pilsen is in the lower west side area of Chicago. Across from Reyes (Guadalupe) Park is the front of an old church. The windows are missing, and through the openings you can see plants growing up from the ground. German words are carved in a stone above the door and I believe translate into Zion Evangelical Lutheran Church. It was built in 1880 by German immigrants who settled in the neighborhood.

Over time, members of the congregation moved away, and the brick church was abandoned in 1956 by its original congregation. In 1979, a devastating fire destroyed the interior and the roof. About two decades later, in 1998, a storm toppled the sidewalls of the once proud church.

The old church was purchased by local resident John Podmajersky Jr. who had plans of demolishing the remains and using the property for an art center. Upon learning of its fate, many of the former congregation met with Podmajersky, sharing their memories of the once beautiful building. Podmajersky was so moved by the love of the old church that he decided to stabilize what remained and converted the land into a garden. Known as the Ghost Church, the steeple continues to tower over the community like a guardian angel.

# Fabyan's Estate and Codebreakers

 Fabyan Forest Preserve
1925 S Batavia Ave,
Geneva, IL 60134
41.87111, -88.31219

The Fabyan Forest Preserve sits along the Fox River south of Geneva. The preserve was once an estate belonging to George and Nelle Fabyan that they named Riverbank. Colonel George, a title he gave himself, gained his vast fortune when he inherited his father's textile business. The Faybans purchased a farmhouse along the Fox River in 1908 and had Frank Lloyd Wright remodel it. The "Villa", as they called it, was the centerpiece of their estate. They created a Japanese garden and a tea house along with a boathouse and a small zoo where they cared for animals, including a bear. On the other side of the river, they built a windmill for grinding grain, which they used to grind grain for the local citizens during World War II.

George had a lot of money and time, which he used to research his belief that Frances Bacon secretly wrote Shakespere's plays. He believed that there were secret codes and ciphers in Shakespere's published works. Across the street from their villa, he built a research laboratory where he hired analysts to dissect the code. Elizebeth and William Friedman were Fabyan's top cryptanalysts (a term coined by William). They believed they had discovered a code for an audio device and Fabyan added an audio research laboratory to his facility.

At the outbreak of World War I, the U.S. Military had limited resources for decrypting secret codes over the newly created radio transmissions. Fabyan donated his resources from his lab to help the war effort. Elizebeth and William Friedman went on to become the government's star codebreakers, helping decipher codes during both World Wars and helping the Coast Guard break codes used by bootleggers during Prohibition.

After the Fabyans' deaths, the estate was purchased by the Kane County Forest Preserve District of Illinois, and it is open to the public to enjoy the Japanese garden and stroll along the river. The Fabyan Villa is now a museum open to the public on weekends through the summer month. The research laboratory still stands across the street but remains private and is closed to the public.

Elizebeth Friedman kept her codebreaking secret throughout her life. Her secret was not revealed until after she died in 1980. Her amazing career and contributions to the United States was highlighted in a PBS episode of *American Experience* titled *The Codebreaker.*

# The Great Train Robbery

Near 13620 Rockland Rd,
Lake Bluff, IL 60044
42.28013, -87.89773

The Town of Rondout sits halfway between Chicago and Milwaukee. The town never grew to be a big metropolis, but several trains passed through the area over the decades. It was one train hauling mail from Chicago in the summer of 1924 that made history.

The four Newton Boys in Texas made a living robbing banks. They claimed to have held-up over eighty banks and were looking for a "Big Score". They met up with some guys from Chicago and learned of a mail train that carried money and bonds. Some of the gang boarded the train in Chicago and managed to force the engineer at gunpoint to stop the train at Rondout where other gang members were waiting in cars to haul away the money. The engineer stopped the train past the crossing and was ordered by the gang to back it up. In the confusion, one of the Chicago guys mistook Wylie "Doc" Newton for a security guard and shot him five times. The gang managed to get Doc into the car with the money and found medical help. The gang absconded with nearly three million dollars; it is considered the largest train heist in U.S. history. Ultimately, it was the accidental shooting that led to the capture and conviction of the gang members. Most of the money was recovered except for $100,000 dollars that Jess Newton buried somewhere Northwest of San Antono, Texas. He could not recall the location because he was drunk at the time he buried it.

Along Illinois Route 176/Rockland Rd. is a historical mark and short section of track that reminds people of the historic train robbery. The Newton Brothers' story was told in the 1998 Matthew McConaughey movie *The Newton Boys.*

# Agriculture Crash Memorial

3497 IL-71,
Marseilles, IL 61341
41.44095, -88.69244

A few miles south of Norway along Illinois Route 71 is the shocking sight of a banged up aircraft with its nose stuck in the ground. It is not a memorial for a plane crash but is marked on the sign in front for the "survivors of the Agricultural Crash of the 1980s". Farming has always been a difficult way to make a living, and in the 1980s it was especially challenging with a period of high inflation, deflated farm land prices, and the grain embargo to the Soviet Union driving down crop prices. Many farms in the 80s were foreclosed on and equipment auctioned off.

In support of the struggling American farmers, musicians Willie Nelson, John Mellencamp and Neil Young organized the Farm Aid benefit concert to raise money for and help family farmers in the United States. The first concert was held in Memorial Stadium in Champaign, Illinois on September 22, 1985 in front of a crowd of 80,000 people.

# LaFluer Grotto

8833 N Kishwaukee Rd,
Stillman Valley, IL 61084
42.14028, -89.20572

N. Kishwaukee Road angles southwest out of Rockford and kind of follows along the Rock River. Traveling along the road near Byron, you will notice a strange and ornate group of concrete structures. The LaFleur Grotto was constructed in

1954 by Joe LaFleur. He prayed to the Virgin Mary for the safe return of his five sons who were fighting in World War II and the Korean War.

Upon their return, he began to build the grotto that stands along the road from concrete and stone from his property. Visitors donated stones, and LaFleur incorporated them into the grotto. A church in Aurora donated a statue of the Virgin Mary that he placed in a central niche. The grotto is an interesting place to stop and admire the creativity of the amateur architect and the gratitude he had for the safe return of his boys.

# The Eternal Native American

Lowden State Park
1411 N River Rd,
Oregon, IL 61061
42.03417, -89.33321

Lowden State Park sits along the Rock River near Oregon, Illinois. In the back of the park overlooking the river is a 48 foot tall statue of a Native American chief with his arms folded as he gazes across the landscape.

Titled The Eternal Indian, but also known as The Black Hawk Statue, it was created by renowned Illinois sculptor Lorado Taft who was raised in Champaign, Illinois. Taft founded the Eagle's Nest Art Colony at the site where the statue now stands. The colony was made up of artists who lived there during the summer months to escape the heat of Chicago.

Taft created the statue in 1911, using concrete supported by steel rods. At the dedication, Taft claimed that the sculpture represents the "unconquerable spirit of Native Americans". It contains motifs from several tribal cultures and was inspired by the Sauk warrior and leader Black Hawk. The statue is said to be the second largest concrete monolithic statue in the world after Christ the Redeemer in Rio de Janeiro. Illinois Governor Frank Lowden had anonymously helped fund the project.

After Eagle's Nest Art Colony vacated the land in 1945, a

portion of the land was utilized to create Lowden State Park. The northern part of the land was given to Northern Illinois Teachers College, now Northern Illinois University, and is now known as the NIU Lorado Taft Field Campus.

In 2009, the statue was added to the National Register of Historic Places. In 2019, the statue underwent a massive restoration, and hopefully, it will stand for generations to come.

# Blackhawk Battlefield Park

# 14109 W Blackhawk Rd, Pearl City, IL 61062
## 42.29564, -89.88179

In a small park in the rolling hills and farmland a few miles southeast of the small town of Kent is a limestone monument. Surrounded by a wrought iron fence, it holds the graves of men killed in Kellogg's Grove during the Black Hawk Wars. In the 1830s, the Native American leader Black Hawk from the Sauk tribe led a band of warriors that attacked American settlers in what is present day Northwestern Illinois and Southwestern Wisconsin. Illinois militia men were sent into the region to defend the settlers' property.

In 1832, two battles took place in the area around the current monument known as Kellogg's Grove. The day after the battle, an Illinois militia company that included a young Abraham Lincoln was sent to bury the dead.

Over time the land where the battle victims were buried became private and in 1886 Stephenson County purchased a small plot of land on a hill which is now Blackhawk Battlefield

Park. The bodies of soldiers in four separate battles were relocated to the park and buried next to the monument.

The area acquired its name when Oliver W. Kellogg built a log cabin on the land in 1827. Wagons hauling lead mined in the region would travel past the Kellogg cabin on a trail that went from Galena to Peoria. Many would stop at Kellogg's place for the night. A replica of the old log cabin stands in the park.

# Leaning Tower of Niles

# 6300 W Touhy Ave, Niles, IL 60714
## 42.01239, -87.78404

If you are traveling down Touhy Ave in the village of Niles northwest of Chicago, you might think you had traveled through a wormhole and ended up in Pisa Italy. A half scale replica of the world famous Leaning Tower of Pisa stands in the village. It was built in 1934 by Robert Ilg to hold water for the pools that his employees could use in his company park. It is believed that he built it to honor the 600th anniversary of the construction of the Leaning Tower of Pisa. He also built it to honor Galileo Galilei, who dropped various objects from the top of the Pisa tower to prove his theory of gravity. A plaque at the base reads: "This tower is dedicated to all who contribute and strive to make this earth and its unlimited resources, materially and scientifically, a better place for mankind."

In 1960, Ilk's descendants donated the tower to the YMCA. The tower was in need of repairs, and in 2015, the village of Niles purchased the tower for $10 from the YMCA and spent more than a half a million dollars on renovations and the surrounding park. It is a symbol of the community and is used as a concert venue during the summertime.

# Ulysses S. Grant Home

500 Bouthillier St,
Galena, IL 61036
42.41124, -90.42437

Illinois is known as the land of Lincoln, but the 18th president, Ulysess S. Grant, had spent some time in the Prairie State. After ending his military career in 1854, he moved his family to the northwestern corner of Illinois in the town of Galena in the spring of 1860. He worked at his father's store with his two brothers.

After the Civil War broke out, he went back into the military, where he worked his way up to commanding the Union Army. After the war, he returned to Galena to a home given to him that was purchased by many prominent citizens of Galena. It is an Italianate style two-story brick home originally built for former City Clerk Alexander J. Jackson. Grant claimed the home as his residence while he was campaigning for president. Throughout the remainder of his life, he owned the house, and after his presidency, he visited the home a few times, the final time in 1880. After Grant's death, his family donated the home to the city of Galena to be used as a memorial for the president who had briefly lived in Galena. The city struggled with funding to maintain the house, and in 1934, it was deeded to the state of Illinois and is now a State Historic Site.

Abraham Lincoln and Ulysses S. Grant were not the only presidents to have lived in Illinois. Ronald Reagan was born in Tampico, Illinois and graduated from Dixon High School. Barack Obama, while born in Hawaii, lived in Chicago for part of his life.

# The Ghost and the Opera House

121 W Van Buren St,
Woodstock, IL 60098
42.31403, -88.44772

Woodstock is about fifty miles northwest of downtown
Chicago. To fans of the movie *Groundhog's Day* starring Bill
Murray, it is a popular town since the town square was used as
a filming location.

Looking over the town square is the Woodstock Opera House. Built in 1889, it was built by the city of Woodstock. The main floor originally housed the city offices, police department, fire department and library. The upper two floors were used as an opera house and community space. A young Orson Wells graced the stage as an actor when he attended Todd School for Boys located in Woodstock. In the 1940s, the stage was also home to the Woodstock Players that included Paul Newman and Tom Bosley. Eventually, the city offices and library moved into separate buildings, and in the 1970s the historic building was renovated. It continues hosting plays and performances.

Like many historic theaters, the building is said to be haunted by superstitious actors and patrons. Legend has it that a beautiful young ballet dancer named Elvira auditioned for a part in a play. Heartbroken after being turned down for the role, she climbed to the top of the opera house bell tower and jumped to her death. They say during performances her spirit sits in the center seat of the balcony. Seat 113 can be seen with its spring loaded seat down during performances with nobody seated in it. Others have heard the sound of a woman singing when someone sings off key.

# Chicago Water Tower

The Chicago water tower after the Great Fire of 1871

806 Michigan Ave,
Chicago, IL 60611
41.89729, -87.6243

Surrounded by skyscrapers is a magical-looking stone structure that appears to be something from a fairy tale. It is made of yellow Joliet limestone and looks like a small castle with a tall tower in the middle. Its stone tower stands 182 feet tall and is not the tallest structure on the Miracle Mile, but it is the oldest. Built in 1869 as part of the water system to supply the growing city of Chicago with water from Lake Michigan, it is one of the few structures to survive the devastating fire in 1871. It still stands as a beacon of hope to the citizens of the Windy City, and the ground level has been converted into an art gallery displaying photographs and paintings.

Legend has it that the tower is haunted by a man that worked the pumps during the Great Fire of 1871. It is said that he continued operating the system until the flames reached the pumping station and instead of being burned alive by the flames, he hung himself in the water tower. I believe it is more of a myth than fact, but according to windycityghosts.com two men did commit suicide by jumping to their deaths from the water tower in 1875 and 1881.

The Chicago water tower is the second-oldest water tower in the United States. The oldest water tower still in use was built in 1860 and stands in Louisville, Kentucky.

# De Immigrant Windmill

111 10th Ave,
Fulton, IL 61252
41.86715, -90.1684

Sailors and boaters traveling along the mighty Mississippi probably think they went through some sort of wormhole and ended up in the Netherlands when they see the massive windmill that stands along the banks in Fulton. The windmill named "De Immigrant" was prefabricated in the Netherlands. It is an authentic replica windmill made of wood and held together by wooden pegs. It stands over one hundred feet tall and is reminiscent of what stands in European countries.

Dutch craftsmen traveled to the Illinois town and assembled the windmill in the summer of 2000. It is fully operational, and the wind powered stone grinding wheels can grind buckwheat, corn, rye, and wheat flours.

# The I & M Canal

Aux Sable Lock and House
4740 Cemetery Rd,
Morris, IL 60450
41.39558, -88.332

The Illinois and Michigan Canal created a waterway from the Great Lakes to the Mississippi River. The 96-mile canal was dug by immigrants in the 1830s. It started in Bridgeport at the Chicago River and went to Lasalle-Peru, where it connected to the Illinois River. The canal was completed in 1848, and mules pulled boats along the canal through seventeen locks. It created an economic boom for the cities and farmers along the canal.

In 1933, the canal was replaced by the Illinois Waterway. The towpaths that were used by mules and their drivers are now used by walkers, runners and cyclists. In 1984, President Ronald Reagan designated the canal the Illinois & Michigan Canal National Heritage Area. It consists of 862 square miles and 60 towns and cities along the historic route. My favorite place is the Aux Sable lock house and lock. It sits in a rural section of the route and is a peaceful place to visit and see an original lock and house that have been restored.

The visitors Center is located on First Street in downtown LaSalle and you can learn more about the I & M Canal at their website www.iandmcanal.org

I hope you will continue
to follow my journey at

www.lostinthestates.com

Other Books by
Mike Sonnenberg

*Lost In Michigan Volumes 1-6*
*Lost In Ohio*
*Lost In Indiana*
*Light From The Birdcage*

Made in the USA
Monee, IL
06 December 2023